CU00847846

THIS WALKER BOOK BELONGS TO:

_____

_____

_____

_____

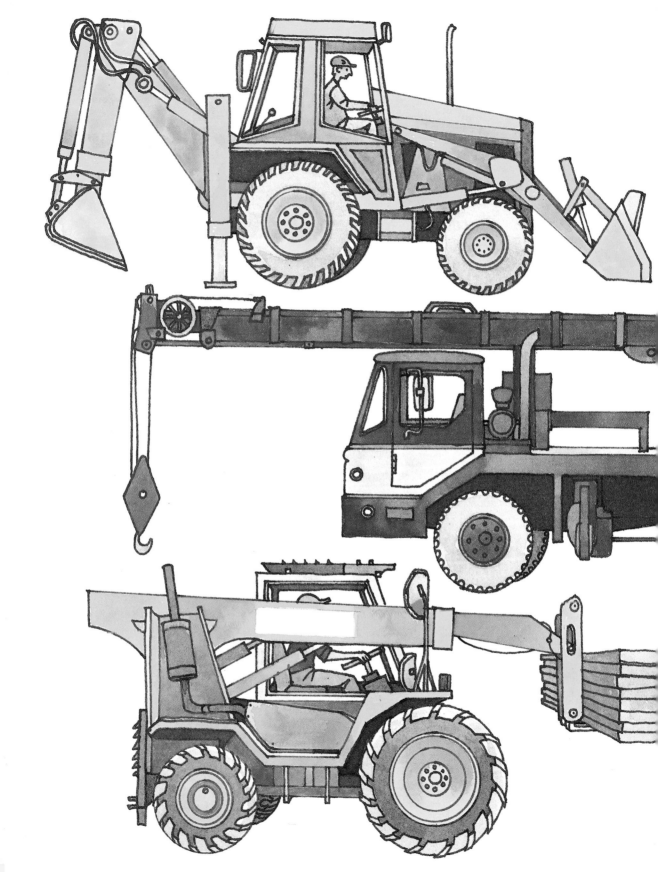

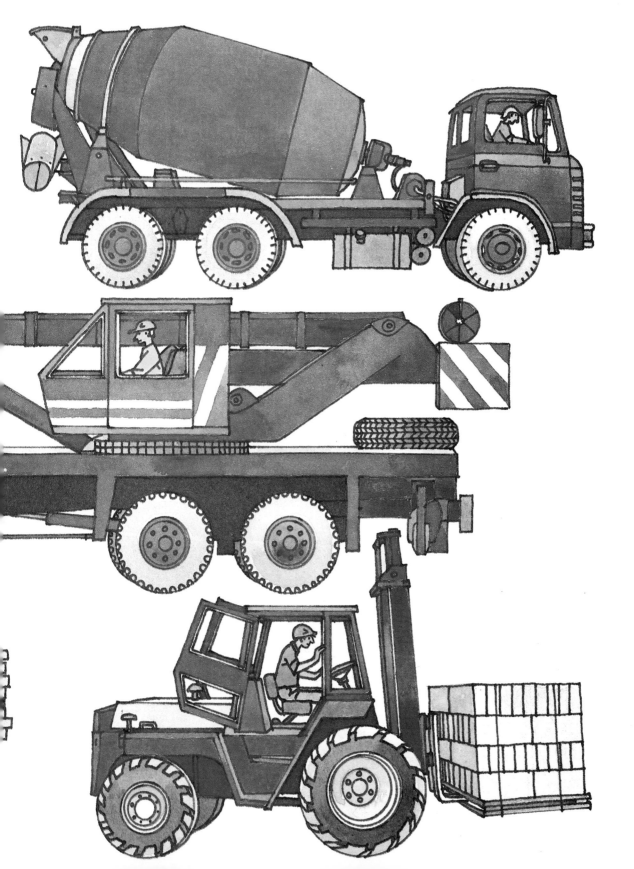

For Mark

First published 1988 by
Walker Books Ltd
87 Vauxhall Walk
London SE11 5HJ

© 1988 Gaynor Chapman

First printed 1988
Printed in Spain by Cayfosa

British Library Cataloguing in Publication Data
Chapman, Gaynor
Building works. — (Machines at work).
1. Building works. — Juvenile literature
I. Title   II. Series
690   TH149

ISBN 0-7445-0917-3

Machines
at Work

BUILDING WORKS

Gaynor Chapman

WALKER BOOKS
LONDON

Before houses are built, an excavator clears the site. The site foreman looks at the architect's plans and sets out where the houses are to go.

A loadall collects the top soil, to be used later for landscaping. A pile-driver noisily bangs piles into the ground to make a firm base for the houses.

A concrete mixer chugs away, mixing the concrete to pour into the hollow piles. In the distance the excavator digs a deep trench for the main sewer.

A backhoe loader digs the foundation trenches which are marked by profile boards.

The concrete mixer brings
extra concrete.

Concrete is poured into a nearby hopper.
Then it is pumped through a pipe to the
foundation trenches. When the concrete
is set, the bricklayers lay the first blocks.

15

A huge mobile crane is getting ready to lift heavy concrete flooring planks.

A hod carrier keeps the bricklayers'
spot boards supplied with mortar.

The bricklayers use thermal blocks to build up the internal walls of the house.

A fork-lift truck takes stacks of bricks from a lorry and lifts them up to the bricklayers on a scaffolding deck.

The loadall brings sections of roof
timbers for carpenters to fix in place.

Tilers put felt, battens and tiles
over the roof timbers.

A lorry collects the builder's skip.

Water, electricity and gas supplies have been set up outside the houses. Inside, plumbers, electricians, joiners, carpenters and plasterers are at work.

The roads and pavements are made up.

Finally, when the other workers have finished, the painters paint the houses. Now people can move in.

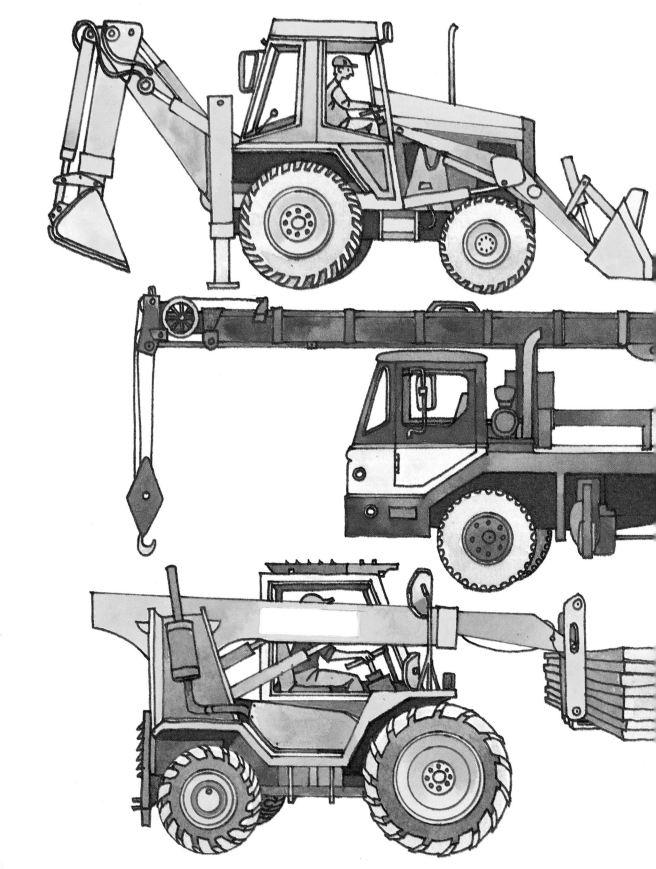

MORE WALKER PAPERBACKS

BABIES' FIRST BOOKS

Jan Ormerod
Baby Books
READING   SLEEPING
DAD'S BACK   MESSY BABY

Marie Wabbes
Little Rabbit
LITTLE RABBIT'S GARDEN
LITTLE RABBIT'S BIRTHDAY
IT'S SNOWING, LITTLE RABBIT
GOOD NIGHT, LITTLE RABBIT

LEARNING FOR FUN
The Pre-School Years

Shirley Hughes
Nursery Collection
NOISY
COLOURS
BATHWATER'S HOT
ALL SHAPES AND SIZES
TWO SHOES, NEW SHOES
WHEN WE WENT TO THE PARK

John Burningham
Concept Books
COLOURS   ALPHABET
OPPOSITES   NUMBERS

Tony Wells   Puzzle Books
PUZZLE DOUBLES
ALLSORTS

PICTURE BOOKS
For The Very Young

Helen Oxenbury
First Picture Books
PLAYSCHOOL   EATING OUT
THE DRIVE   OUR DOG
THE CHECK-UP   THE VISITOR
THE BIRTHDAY PARTY
GRAN AND GRANDPA
THE DANCING CLASS

Pam Zinnemann-Hope
& Kady MacDonald Denton
The Ned Books
TIME FOR BED NED
LET'S PLAY BALL NED
FIND YOUR COAT NED
LET'S GO SHOPPING NED

Niki Daly Storytime
LOOK AT ME!
JUST LIKE ARCHIE
MONSTERS ARE LIKE THAT

Jan Ormerod
CHICKEN LICKEN

Jill Murphy
FIVE MINUTES' PEACE